Hélio Oiticica: Secret Poetics

translated from Portuguese
and with an introduction by
Rebecca Kosick

afterword by **Pedro Erber**

Soberscove Press & Winter Editions, 2023

Hélio Oiticica: Secret Poetics

ISBN 978-1-940190-32-7
First Edition, 2023 — 1500 copies

Soberscove Press, Chicago, IL (soberscove.com)
Winter Editions, Brooklyn, NY (wintereditions.net)

Library of Congress Cataloging-in-Publication Data

Names: Oiticica, Hélio, 1937-1980, author. | Kosick, Rebecca, translator, writer of introduction. | Erber, Pedro R., 1975- writer of afterword.
Title: Secret poetics / Hélio Oiticica ; translated from Portuguese and with an introduction by Rebecca Kosick ; afterword by Pedro Erber.
Other titles: Poética secreta. English
Description: First edition. | Chicago, IL : Soberscove Press ; Brooklyn, New York : Winter Editions, 2023. | Includes bibliographical references.
Identifiers: LCCN 2023019516 | ISBN 9781940190327 (paperback)
Subjects: LCSH: Oiticica, Hélio, 1937-1980--Translations into English. | LCGFT: Poetry.
Classification: LCC PQ9698.25.I85 P6413 2023 | DDC 869.1/42--dc23/eng/20230524
LC record available at https://lccn.loc.gov/2023019516

Obra publicada com o apoio do Ministério das Relações Exteriores do Brasil em conjunto com a Fundação Biblioteca Nacional – Ministério da Cultura. / Published with the support of the Brazilian Ministry of Foreign Affairs in collaboration with the Brazilian National Library Foundation – Ministry of Culture.

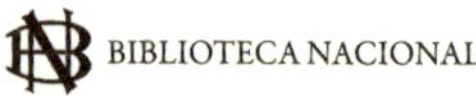

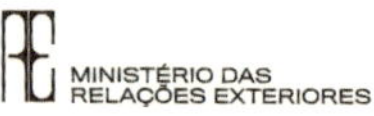

CONTENTS

Hélio Oiticica: Secret Poet

by Rebecca Kosick

Between 1964 and 1966, the Brazilian artist Hélio Oiticica (Rio de Janeiro, 1937–1980) wrote a series of lyrical poems and accompanying reflections on poetry under the title *Poética secreta* (Secret Poetics). These poems, written by hand on a pad of paper, were composed at a turning point in Oiticica's life, directly following the death of his father and just as Oiticica was beginning a productive collaboration with dancers from Rio's Mangueira Samba School that would influence his artwork for years to come. Though the poems do not express overt political commitments, they were also written in the early years of Brazil's military dictatorship, which began in 1964 and would last for twenty-one years. The themes Oiticica attends to in these writings include pleasure, pain, embodied and sensory experience, signification, the limits of expression, memory, longing, and love as physical act and feeling.

Secret Poetics seems to have been a largely private undertaking for Oiticica, and this may be one reason for the use of the word "secret" in the title. These poems were never published as a book, nor incorporated into Oiticica's artworks as some other texts were. And Oiticica did not consider himself to be a poet. In fact, it was a title he emphatically disavowed in comments he recorded in a notebook just as he began writing *Secret Poetics*. His refusal of the status of "poet" could suggest his timidity at working in a new form or, as the scholar Federico Coehlo has argued, it could also signal Oiticica's "extreme respect" for poetry.[1] Whether Oiticica was a poet or an artist working with poetry, it's clear that writing *Secret Poetics* provided him with a new method for exploring some of his broader aesthetic commitments from the 1960s, especially sensory participation.

***

Over the course of his life, Oiticica worked in a variety of media—painting, sculpture, film, installation art, performance, participatory art, experimental writing, theory. He engaged with poetry and writing through many of these practices, but just as he did not consider himself to be a poet, he has not been known as one either. While his work is to some degree "unclassifiable,"[2] it is in the spheres of the visual arts—or the "plastic" arts, as they are known in Brazil—that Oiticica's varied aesthetic output has been primarily received, enframed, and celebrated. His art practice included anti-institutional gestures, but Oiticica's work is now fully embedded in art-world institutions and has been shown widely in the most established galleries and museums. The last decade has seen a number of significant retrospectives in the United States, Germany, Brazil, Argentina, and the United Kingdom, and Oiticica is now "widely regarded as one of Brazil's leading artists of the twentieth century

1 Coelho, "Livro ou livro-me," 109.

2 Small, *Folding the Frame*, 3.

and a touchstone for much contemporary art made since the 1960s."[3]

Oiticica is well known for his participation in the concrete art movement, a mid-twentieth-century branch of geometric abstraction that was linked to design via figures such as the Swiss architect, painter, and designer Max Bill. Though concrete art was international in scope, it flourished in Brazil following a showing of Bill's work at the 1951 São Paulo Biennial, and adherents grouped themselves into two geographically and aesthetically affiliated clusters known as Grupo Ruptura (literally "Rupture Group"), based in São Paulo, and Grupo Frente ("Front [as in wartime or the avant-garde] Group"), based in Rio de Janeiro. Oiticica was part of the second group, formed by artist Ivan Serpa and counting among its members other artists now known internationally, such as Lygia Clark and Lygia Pape, as well as Aluísio Carvão, Vicent Ibberson, João José da Silva Costa, Carlos Val, and Décio Vieira. While the artists involved weren't absolute in their orientation toward a shared aesthetic, their version of concrete art tended to use simple geometric shapes and a limited chromatic range. Many of Oiticica's paintings from the concrete era are illustrative of this tendency, and resisted the use of paint as a tool for representative expression, orienting viewers' attention instead toward form, surface, and color.

---

3 Lisson Gallery, "Press Release Hélio Oiticica."

Oiticica's early paintings, such as the self-referentially named *Grupo Frente* series (see figure 1), are characteristic of this approach, employing a selection of colors arranged in a geometric layout made of squares and rectangles set at 90-degree angles. Other paintings include forms such as pentagons, circles, and lines that zig-zag up the surface as though tracing a set of stairs. While the *Grupo Frente* series generally positions shapes at right angles, Oiticica's paintings increasingly jostled the forms on their surfaces as the 1950s continued. Works from the 1957–1958 series *Metaesquemas* (Metaschemes), for example, "exhibit an idiosyncratic principle of rotational symmetry in which shapes appear to slip or slide against one another in a floating lateral space."[4]

There is a suggestion of movement, even dance, in the *Metaesquemas*, but later artworks would literalize this proposition, pushing the largely two-dimensional tendencies of concrete painting in further directions: namely, outward. Oiticica and others involved with Grupo Frente turned toward three-dimensional structures that, "aspired to overcome the plane."[5] These works also invited new modes of interactive apprehension, beyond mere ocular appreciation—they were meant to be walked around, ducked under, touched, and opened. This shift in approach may be traced as far back

---

4 Small, 35.

5 Amor, "From Work to Frame," 25.

as 1959, when Oiticica and an interdisciplinary group of artists-poets-theorists including Clark, Pape, and poet Ferreira Gullar, launched the "neoconcrete" movement, which would last roughly five years until the onset of Brazil's military dictatorship. In a manifesto published in the Sunday supplement of the national newspaper, the *Jornal do Brasil*, the self-proclaimed neoconcretists offered a vision for what we might now call an intermedia art. Rejecting the "rationalism" that informed concrete art, the neoconcrete group pursued a more relational and intuitive approach to art that involved greater participation of the audience. This aim was in contrast with concrete poetry as well. Concrete poets such as São Paulo's Noigandres group—Haroldo de Campos, Augusto de Campos, and Décio Pignatari—prized "an immediate form of communication."[6] But neoconcretists were interested in duration, and in extending the apparently instantaneous apprehension of a concrete poem into an aesthetic experience that would last, an impetus identifiable in Oiticica's *Secret Poetics* as well.

From a theoretical point of view, the participatory developments of neoconcretism not only dissolved the distance between spectator and art object but collapsed the very binaries structuring the differentiation of subject and object, inviting viewers into the work of art and activating the art object by way of its relation with sensing human bodies. This turn toward sensation and interaction was informed by the group's study of

6 de Campos, *Novas*, 243.

phenomenology and aesthetics under the guidance of the critic and intellectual Mário Pedrosa,[7] and engagement with the work of Maurice Merleau-Ponty, Susanne Langer, Ernst Cassirer, and Henri Bergson, among others. The neoconcretists understood the work of art as "a being" whose meaning would "flourish" via phenomenological encounter with its audience-participants.[8] This was opposed to a concept of art that understands the artwork—a painting, a sculpture—as an object distinct from the perceiving subject.

Even after his involvement in neoconcretism, Oiticica continued to pursue an interactive approach to art. Pedro Erber, who contributes the closing essay of this volume, notes that participation became a primary concern for Oiticica with the *Bólides* (Fireballs) series (see figures 3, 4, and 7), a set of works involving interactive boxes and containers that the artist pursued between 1963 and 1967, a period that overlapped with his writing of *Secret Poetics*.[9] The pieces in this series invited audience interaction, allowing "viewers" to, for example, open drawers; reach into a various kinds of receptacles; handle sacks of pigment; touch dirt or water. Later examples of Oiticica's participatory works included wearable, cape-like garments known as

---

7 Gullar, *in Conversation*, 37–38.

8 Ibid., 37.

9 Erber, *Breaching the Frame*, 114.

Parangolés (see figure 5).[10] Guy Brett describes these as "complex networks of different materials and colours, with hidden pockets and bags containing colour-powders to be touched by the wearer. Polythene, gauze, sacking, silk, muslin, etc. surround the spectator in sensual modulations of colour."[11] By this point in Oiticica's practice, then, the spectator wasn't really just spectating anymore.

***

The interactive and relational proposals of neoconcretism played out across both visual and verbal creations, blurring the line between the poetic and the plastic arts. Neoconcrete poetry, like neoconcrete art, took up the challenges of a sensorial, participatory form, resulting in works like Ferreira Gullar's *poemas-objetos* (object poems) which readers could physically manipulate—for example, by opening boxes or hinges, or moving a part of a structure on and off of its base. These objects contained very limited verbal language—only one word—thus elevating the importance of sensorial engagement with the poem.

During the late '50s and early '60s, Oiticica collaborated with Gullar, including on 1959's *Poema*

---

10 The title of this series is a bit of Carioca slang that, per Vincent Katz, is "associated with the malandro figure—a well-dressed ne'er-do-well who lives off women, his style and wits." (Katz, "Living Colour")

11 Brett, *Kinetic Art*, 67.

enterrado (Buried Poem), which the pair constructed at the site of a house Oiticica's father, José Oiticica Filho, was building near the Rio neighborhood of Jardim Botânico. As in Gullar's object poetry, this poem consisted of only a single word—"rejuvenesça" (rejuvenate)—but the poem was the size of an underground room, inviting the entry of readers' whole bodies. The *Buried Poem* relates to the *Penetráveis* (Penetrables) series that Oiticica worked on between 1961 and 1980, a series that also overlapped with the writing of *Secret Poetics*. There are clearly links between the Gullar-Oiticica *Buried Poem* collaboration and Oiticica's *Penetrables*. These were, as the Museum of Modern Art in Rio de Janeiro describes, "human-scaled structures composed of booths and banners made of different fabrics and painted wooden boards or other materials, which can be penetrated, traversed and manipulated by living bodies, in an informal and spontaneous way."[12] Two of the most famous *Penetrables* are included in Oiticica's *Tropicália* installation (see figure 2), which was first exhibited in Rio's Museum of Modern Art in 1967 and lent its title to the musical movement of the same name.

Notably, the *Tropicália* installation included poetry too, but its use of language was distinct from the minimal, nondiscursive approach typical of neoconcrete poetry. The poems included in the work by the poet Roberta Camila Salgado were brief, but not to the degree of Gullar's one-word poems. They were object-

12 "Penetráveis, 1961-1980."

integrated, in that they were painted/inscribed on objects placed throughout the multi-structured *Tropicália* installation—objects like "brick blocks, ceramic roofing tiles, cardboard sheets, styrofoam and wooden boards."[13] But *Tropicália*'s poems didn't propose the kind of tight isomorphism of form and content that was materialized by concrete and neoconcrete poems alike (for instance, in one of Gullar's object poems, the single word *não* [no] is printed inside a circle in stop-sign red, the word and the color indicative of each other). Salgado's poems were part of *Tropicália*'s larger participatory structure, which invited whole-body interaction, but, as opposed to neoconcrete poetry, Salgado's poems made external references that prominently included "themes of her time, such as oppression and the growing dismantling of public space, as a result of the dictatorship that had been established in Brazil in 1964."[14] *Tropicália* included other text that conveyed similarly content-rich and politically inflected messages, such as the words "A PUREZA É UM MITO" (PURITY IS A MYTH) stenciled across the top of one of the interior walls of a penetrable structure within the work.

---

13 Masseno, "Os poemobjetos de Roberta Camila Salgado," 180.

14 Ibid., 186.

***

Tropicália and the *Bólides* both incorporated poetry, but for Oiticica, poetry and the plastic arts served different functions, something which was underscored in *Secret Poetics*. These lyric poems act as a material archive for a set of subjective experiences that take place outside of the poems themselves. Where Oiticica's works of plastic art allow human subjects to actually touch and interact with them—to sense them—the poems instead recount experiences of sensation that are not actual to the moment of reading. Nevertheless, each "half" of Oiticica's work during this era—poetic and plastic—served a purpose for the artist and for the participatory ambitions of his practice. If the plastic works enable actual sensations, these sensations are brief and fleeting, over as soon as the participant takes off the *Parangolé*. The poems, on the other hand, don't offer these actual experiences, but have the potential to extend what's fleeting in the form of a record, or a recollection. Oiticica comments in 1964 that "a moment of pleasure can become eternal in memory," and all throughout *Secret Poetics* are furious obsessions over memories of sensory experiences including lust, disgust, pleasure, and pain. How to keep these experiences alive is a question that motivates Oiticica's turn to poetry.

I first came across these poems when I was researching Oiticica's relationship to neoconcrete poetry for my book *Material Poetics in Hemispheric America*. Facsimiles of the original handwritten poems are (at the time of this writing) held in a digital archive, though they were originally written by the artist in blue ink on sheets of yellow paper. Accompanying the poems is a notebook addendum, also now in digital facsimile. In the notebook, the artist's reflections on the lyric and his intentions for *Secret Poetics* are recorded in similarly colored ink on sheets of white lined paper, bound by a three-hole punch. The poems are written out carefully, though Oiticica's notebook comments—composed on July 21, 1964—appear to have been laid down more quickly, and it's sometimes difficult to decipher his writing.

These digital versions of the handwritten texts may be all that remains of *Secret Poetics*. The Projeto Hélio Oiticica, which was set up by the artist's family after his death, suffered a fire in 2009, and although not all of the documents and works were destroyed, the task of re-sorting and archiving the materials that remain is still underway. Whether the handwritten texts are still there or not, the events of 2009 reveal the fact that, like all material objects, documents of this sort are at risk of being lost. Publishing these poems nearly 75 years after Oiticica first wrote *Secret Poetics* is an act, however partial, that follows Oiticica's understanding of the lyric: as a way, like memory, for the temporary to endure.

The making of this book has been impacted by experiences and materials that have pressed themselves through time and language. Reproducing the Portuguese originals in facsimile allows us to see the physicality of the pages Oiticica originally wrote on, as well as his handwriting, which highlights the fact that these texts were produced in intimate, rather than commercial, circumstances. It also highlights the hybrid genre of Oiticica's poetry and poetic writing. This is poetry, but these are also notes, a kind of diary—documents of a contemporary artist's developing ideas and thinking in the form of poetry. What we see here are pages written by the artist in real time, marked with the date of their writing—the mark of his touch on the page, a record of his hand and not just his head. This is the "sedimentação da lembrança" (sedimentation or, as I've translated it, *sediment* of memory) that Oiticica references in the poem dated August 5, 1964—what is left behind.

My translations are shaped not only by the physicality of the original texts, but by other aspects of Oiticica's material practices as well, including his work with language. For instance, I have sought ways of rearticulating in English the sonic wordplay that Oiticica frequently deploys within the collection. Though these are not concrete poems, they play with words in ways typical of concrete, and some neoconcrete, poetry—emphasizing lexical similarities, regardless of whether an etymological tie underlies this bond or not. For example, in the poem from March 22, 1966, I have taken Oiticica's lead and translated the sonic resonance of the Portuguese *o sono* (the sleep) and *o sonho* (the dream) less literally as "the drift-off" and "the dream," in order to generate interlingual resemblances where English affords them.

Beyond Oiticica's work with language and its materiality—as sounds, as marks on the page, as pages—his "plastic" practices have also informed my translations here. Many poems in *Secret Poetics* share significant relationships with artworks that Oiticica also made in the 1960s. Though these works of art were generally made after the poems in question, my translations are coming after them both, so, in addition to the actual text of the poems themselves, I have taken these artworks into account.

One of the most striking "resemblances" between the poetic and plastic branches of Oiticica's practice circles around this brief poem from August 23, 1964:

> Water,
> glassy surface,
> plunge.

This three-liner relates directly to *B47 Bólide caixa* (Fireball Box) *22 "Mergulho do corpo"* (figure 4), a water tank Oiticica made in 1966/67 whose surface looks, indeed, glassy. *Mergulho* means "dive" or "plunge," but the conventional English translation for the work's subtitle is "Plunge of the Body." If I had been translating this poem without consulting the artwork, I might have gone with "dive" instead of "plunge." I grew up around lakes, and that's the image that comes to me first when I read the poem. This imaginative inclination toward "dive" is perhaps solidified by a potential intertextual dialogue Oiticica's poem establishes with one of the world's most well-known and most translated poems, Matsuo Bashō's seventeenth-century frog haiku, in whose final line we hear the splash of a frog into a pond introduced in the first line. We don't know for sure that a reference to Bashō was deliberate, but we know haiku is a form Oiticica was working with at the time—his notebook reflections on *Secret Poetics* include three haiku-style poems—and there are thematic connections that link the two poems across time.

A frog in a pond could jump, plunge, or dive. But most importantly, that frog has the potential for full-body immersion. In the artwork subtitled *Plunge of the Body*, Oiticica's human participants do not have this potential. The water basin that is the artwork is about two feet square and less than two feet deep, hence: *no diving*; it's more of a plunge-of-the-hands-sized tub. Maybe the feet or an elbow, the head if you're adventurous. As I worked on another iteration of Oiticica's short poem in English, I needed a word that signaled the participatory nature of this artwork as much as the poems that informed it, a word whose travels under water didn't necessarily assume the size of a whole person. So: plunge.

The final two poems of *Secret Poetics* are concerned with a different kind of participatory experience: the contradictions of Eros's pleasure-pain axis. In the first of these, Oiticica writes of the "chicote que acaricia"—the "whip that caresses," or, as I've translated it here to echo the alliterations throughout *Secret Poetics,* the "lash that lavishes." Oiticica's love-lash can be understood in retrospect as relating to what he elsewhere calls "the fury of the participatory relation."[15] In a letter to Lygia Clark from 1968 (just two years after the final poem of *Secret Poetics* was written), Oiticica describes seeing Caetano Veloso—one of the most well-known musicians of the Tropicália movement—being "totally devoured, in an almost physical sense," by "millions of students, adolescents, in an incredible fury."[16] We might read this scene as a familiar fan reaction of the Beatlemania variety, but for Oiticica, it speaks to the participatory relation between the artist and the audience. Oiticica writes that "giving does not push aside the taking: on the contrary, it stimulates it, in an erotic way too."[17] For him, participation, along with the artistic letting go that it entails, "confuses and liberates truly unpredictable forces."[18]

These forces are physical, at the level of the animal urge realized, and, per Oiticica, this is what an artist invites for himself in participation:

> This is why there is this unbearable experience [*vivência*] of ours, of being deflowered, of possession, as if he, the spectator, would say: "Who are you? What do I care if you created this or not? Well, I am here to modify everything, this

15 Clark and Oiticica, "Letters 1968-69," 112.

16 Ibid.

17 Ibid., 112–113.

18 Ibid.

> unbearable shit that proposes dull experiences, or good ones, libidinous, fuck you, and all of this because I devour you, and then I shit you out; what is of interest only I can experience and you will never evaluate what I feel and think, the lust that devours me." And the artist comes out of it in tatters. But it is good.[19]

We can see this devouring lust in the final two poems of *Secret Poetics*, where "want" is wound together with "bile" and violence.

> I want: I don't have,
> impossible to stop wanting
>
> — all there is is my want;
>
> the nontaste,
> invisible sword in the body;
> bile.

If we take the poem on its own, we might understand it as recounting an individualized experience of lust, and maybe attribute it to Oiticica himself. If we think about these poems as being in dialogue with his participatory practices in the plastic arts—and as documents of the artist's theorizing of those practices in the form of poetry—then we see that the speaker is not (just)

19 Ibid., 111.

Oiticica, but rather throngs of lusting spectators, their want activated by participation. Furthermore, there may be no "speaker" at all, because the poem—and the participatory relation—extends experience indefinitely and unknowably across all individual iterations of experience itself. The "I" of this poem isn't a self, but a placeholder for the selves that might come to the poem. And the artist can never get a read on all of them.

This is why the spectator Oiticica imagines in his letter to Clark can say to the artist "you will never evaluate what I feel and think." The artist can stage a participatory relation, but what the participants feel—fury, lust, or otherwise—can't be totally revealed to the artist. This may be one reason why, in this poem, the taste (*paladar*) isn't specified. The artist can't know what a reader tastes, and as the translator, neither can I. Instead, there is a "nontaste." There is an "invisible sword," but the feel as it stabs you—well, that's down to you.

Understanding the sensations of the poetry as extending from us (the participants) rather than the poet (artist) is also a helpful way to think about the presence of a "her" in the final poem:

> wait,
> wait for her;
>   oh,
>   love

The line that I have translated into English as "wait for her" is, in Portuguese, *esperança dela,* which literally means "hope/wait of her" or "her hope/wait." I have it as "wait," not "hope," in order to keep as close as possible to Oiticica's root repetition of *espera/esperança* (wait/hope). "Wait for her" suggests that it's the speaker who is waiting, in the sense of "a wait that derives from her"—an unwanted wait, a can't-stand-it wait, a fury of unfulfilled desire. But the "her" also perplexed me, knowing that Oiticica was gay. This does not necessarily exclude a possibility of heterosexual longing, or a feminized object of affection, but as the scholar Pauline Bachmann has stressed, the period in which *Secret Poetics* was written also coincides with Oiticica's self-discovery and profound early sexual experiences with other men.[20] Bachmann suggests that this is partly why the collection as a whole is preoccupied with erotic experience, and that these preoccupations, like a subtext, in turn inform Oiticica's then-growing investment in sensorial experience more generally.[21]

Portuguese is a gendered language—its nouns are grammatically male or female. "Her" could refer to another non-person female noun, like the "caress" a few lines up, or lust, or fury. But considering Oiticica's interest in the participatory relation, I read these lines not as a fictional depiction of heterosexual desire, but

---

20 Bachmann, "A poesia como subtexto," 175.

21 Ibid.

as an opening to readers' partaking in the erotics of the poem—a wait for or of her, a wait where we are her, a wild drumming longing of her own, wherever we might find it, and however we might embody it, ourselves. In Oiticica's "her," I read "the lust that devours me," or any of us.

In devouring, there is a further allusion to the metaphor of anthropophagy (cannibalism) that Brazilian writer Oswald de Andrade mobilized in his 1928 "Manifesto antropófago" (Cannibalist manifesto), an important text for the Brazilian avant-garde. This metaphor has been read as advocating "the critical devouring of the universal cultural legacy,"[22] meaning that Brazilian artists should consume, digest, and "shit out"—as in Oiticica's description of the spectator—new and nonderivative Brazilian cultural creations. This idea was later applied to translation by the twentieth-century São Paulo–based concrete poet Haroldo de Campos, who writes of "translation as transgressive appropriation and hybridism (or cross-breeding) as the dialogic practice of expressing the other and expressing oneself through the other, under the sign of difference."[23]

Though we might think about interlingual translation as an inevitably boundary-transgressing activity, in these translations, I have not taken de Campos's approach explicitly. Instead, I have for the most

22 de Campos, "Tradition, Translation, Transculturation," 14.

23 Ibid.

part deferred to patterns and preferences established by Oiticica's poetics and have taken liberties only as necessitated or encouraged by his use of language there, in Portuguese, and what possibilities we find for language over here, in English. But de Campos's phrase—"expressing the other and expressing oneself through the other, under the sign of difference"—is useful for understanding Oiticica's deep deference to his spectator-participants. If the work of participatory art, a work like *Plunge of the Body*, is a container that invites and catalyzes experience, then these poems are containers too. Not in the sense of keeping in, but in the sense of holding space—for the unknowable, and therefore *secret* experiences we can fill them with. The *nontaste* that Oiticica expresses—that's where we come in.

Notebook

21-Julho-64

lírica

Começo aqui e hoje o que chamarei de "poética secreta", ou seja, aquilo que me expressarei no sentido verbal, poèticamente. O verdadeiro lírico é imediato, isto é, o imediato que se torna eterno na expressão poética lírica, exatamente o pólo oposto da minha obra plástica, tôda orientada para uma expressão que exclue o passageiro, os acidentes mesquinhos, apesar de os abarcar. Está, porém, 'acima' dêles, em plano ideal, o que não acontece na lírica, em poesia, pois o que poderia ser mesquinho, o dia a dia, torna-se vivência e eterniza-se no poema (se bem que o lírico se oriente também para um plano ideal, mas o "passageiro" é que constitue o cerne do seu material). 'Secreta', é o que quero, pois que não sou poeta, mas uma imperiosa necessidade me leva à expressão verbal. Quando me encontro, aqui, nas vivências cotidianas, que nas obras procuro construir idealmente (vivência da obra transformando as vivências do cotidiano), aqui essas vivências constroem o pensamento ideal, e orientam-no em novas perspectivas, numa outra visão, desconcertante por certo, principalmente agora, para mim. A experiência do que se convencionou chamar "vida" toca aqui o seu dedo no ideal das aspirações, da liberdade da vontade, mostra certas vias, certas intuições surgem em botão, florescência do cotidiano. Os poemas que surgirão aqui ten-

July 21, 1964

Here and today, I begin what I will call "secret poetics," or, those things I will express verbally, poetically. The true lyric is immediate, that is, immediacy that becomes eternal in lyrical poetic expression, exactly the polar opposite of my plastic work, which is all oriented toward expression that excludes fleeting, inconsequential accidents, despite embracing them. It is, nevertheless, "above" them, on an ideal level. That doesn't happen in the lyric, in poetry, for what might be inconsequential, day-to-day, becomes experience and is eternalized in the poem (it may be that the lyric also orients itself toward the ideal, but the "fleeting" is what constitutes the core of its material). "Secret" is what I want because I am not a poet, although an urgent necessity leads me to verbal expression. When I find myself here in everyday experiences, which I try to construct ideally in my artwork (the experience of the work transforming everyday experiences), here those experiences construct ideal thought, and orient it toward new perspectives, toward another view, disconcerting for sure, especially now, for me. The experience of what we conventionally call "life" here presses its finger on ideal aspirations, on free will. It shows certain paths, certain intuitions begin to bud, the flowering of the everyday. The poems that will emerge here

dem a sintetizar essas vivências — fluem, assim o quero, no espaço linear dessas fô-
lhas, em continuidade.

Só,
que não era só,
no tempo.

Ave,
ó beleza!,
que já é lembrança.

Belo,
o belo,
sem conceito.

tend to synthesize those experiences—they'll flow, I hope, in the linear space of these pages, continuously.

  Just,
that it wasn't just,
in time

Bird,
O beauty!,
that's already a memory.

Beautiful,
  the beautiful,
  conceptless.

Certa vez li, em Krishnamurti, algo sobre a memória de fatos vividos, simplesmente a "memória"; dizia ele ser essa memória, a lembrança, uma vivência incompleta, um momento não vivido integralmente: a lembrança seria uma via para a sua completação. Pensava eu então ser isso um "tempo morto", as lembranças seriam falhas na vida, casos não vividos. Vejo, porém, que interpretei mal o que Krishnamurti quis dizer; se há a lembrança, a memória, para a completação de vivências, não há um "tempo morto" intermediário, que complete a lembrança, mas uma verdadeira "vivência da transformabilidade do tempo". O tempo da memória, o presente-passado, possui a sua vivência própria e tensa: o que se quer, que passou e fica na lembrança, vem para ser completado dentro dela mesma: dor traz dor, o prazer perdido traz novo prazer; o que chamamos "saudade" não é uma dor, mas um prazer que se repõe na transformabilidade da lembrança. Um momento de prazer pode-se tornar eterno pela memória — a necessidade da sua repetição indefinida e a não consecução dessa repetição tornam-o incompleto, transformando-o, como a toda vivência incompleta, em lembrança.

I once read in Krishnamurti something about the memory of lived events, simply "memory." He said that memory, a recollection, was an incomplete experience, a moment not fully lived: that the remembering would be a path to its own completion. I thought then that this would be "dead time," that memories would be gaps in life, unlived events. But I see that I had misinterpreted what Krishnamurti meant; if a recollection, a memory, is there to complete experience, there isn't an intermediary "dead time" that constitutes the memory, but a true "experience of the transformability of time." The time of memory, the present-past, possesses its own tense experience: what is wanted, what happened and remains in memory, comes to be completed within itself: pain brings pain, lost pleasure brings new pleasure, what we call "*saudade*" isn't pain, but pleasure that replenishes itself in the transformability of memory. A moment of pleasure can be made eternal by memory—the need for it to repeat indefinitely, and the interminability of this repetition, makes it incomplete, transforming it, like all incomplete experiences, into memory.

Hélio Oiticica

Poética Secreta

ADENDO 1 (ver notebook respectivo)

Hélio Oiticica

Secret Poetics

Addendum 1 (see respective notebook)

AD·1

1

UNIVERSIDADE DO BRASIL

4-Agôsto-64

Hélio Oiticica

O cheiro,
tato novo,
recomeçar dos sentidos,
absorção,
lembrança,
oh!,
virá o que,
far-se-á,
virá a ser,
será
punhado de futuro,
apreensão.

August 4, 1964

The smell,
new touch,
restarting of the senses,
            absorption,
            memory,
oh!,
      come what may,
      what shall be,
      will become,
      will be
fistful of future,
                  apprehension.

AD 1

2

A sombra,
possível reencontro,
antigo encontro,
só ;
ei!
beleza perdida
há tanto querida,
requerida,
só ;
secreto anseio
inexprimível,
indizível,
só, na incomunicabilidade.

ZW 4-8-64

The shadow,
possible re-encounter,
old encounter,
just;
    hey!
        lost beauty
there's so much, dear,
needed,
just;
    secret desire
inexpressible,
unspeakable,
just, in the incommunicable.

August 4, 1964

AD 1

O que foi,
ficou,
sedimentação da lembrança.

JCO 5-8-64

What was,
stayed,
sediment of memory.

August 5, 1964

AD 1

A espera,
frieza,
ir e vir,
naturalidade do porvir.

O rio que corre,
segrêdo,
continua,
a procura.

Oh!
porque a impossibilidade?
A imagem,
memória,
o tato,
contato do côrpo.

FCO 5-8-64

The wait,
cold,
coming and going,
the natural of the will-be.

The river that runs,
secret,
continues,
the search.

Oh!
    Why the impossible?
The image,
memory,
the tactile,
contact with the body.

August 5, 1964

AD 1 3

Água,
superfície vítrea,
mergulho.

NO 23-8-64

Water,
glassy surface,
plunge.

August 23, 1964

AD 1

4

A terra,
o marron, o ocre,
passado;
a dança,
o cosmos, no ritmo,
mito.

JLO 23-8-64

The earth,
the brown, the ochre,
past;
the dance,
the cosmos, in rhythm,
myth.

August 23, 1964

AD 1

O fiar,
fazer-se (desfazer-se),
a implicação da memória,
lembrança,
o esquecimento ou o não-esquecer,
persistência do passado,
futuro,
a vivência do agora,
sempre ser,
oh!
o que?,
o sempre,
o nada,
o fogo.

1-9-64

The spinning,
becoming (unbecoming),
the implication of memory,
remembering,
the forgetting or the unforgetting,
persistence of the past,
future,
the experience of the now,
always being,
                    oh!
oh what?,
               the always,
the nothing,
                    the fire.

September 1, 1964

AO 1

Pele négra,
contacto do agora,
visão do sempre,
amor;

escuro,
visão do tato,
contacto;

veludo,.
carícia do tato,
o sempre no sempre,
abraço;

o braço,
côrpo e entrelaço,
lábio;

tato do corpo,
mãos,
cruzar as mãos,
o sono

o sonho.

hp 22-3-66

Black skin,
contact with the now,
vision of the always,
love;

            dark,
vision of the tactile,
contact.

velvet,
caress of the touch,
the always in the always,
embrace;

the arm,
body and I interlace,
lip;

feel of the body,
hands,
crossing hands,
the drift-off

the dream.

March 22, 1966

AD 1

Presença,
alternância da imagem,
a pele,
a côr,
o que se não vê;

Atração,
objeto do afeto,
chegada,
partida,
trânsito da imagem;

Paradoxo,
a presença que é,
a ausência é,
conhecer o não conhecido;

Eternidade de ser,
o que não é já é,
oh,
que fazer,
outra vez a imagem,
vista,
não vista,
imprescindível!

HO 23-3-66

Presence,
alternation of the image,
the skin,
the color,
the unseen;

Attraction,
object of affection,
coming,
going,
transit of the image;

Paradox,
the presence that is,
the absence is,
knowing the unknown;

Eternity of being,
what is not is already,
oh,
    to make
the image again,
seen,
unseen,
indispensable!

March 23, 1966

AD 1

O gôsto amargo do que é dôce
senti,
sinto,
o chicote que acaricia; —
dúvida;

o amargor da carícia,
o tempo,
passar o tempo,
espera,
esperança dela;
oh,
o amor
amargor,
flor de fel,
o não-mel,
dor da memória,
lembrança do que se quer;

quero: não tenho,
impossível deixar de querer

— tudooque é é o meu querer;
o não-paladar,
espada invisível no côrpo;
fel.

AD 30-3-66

The bitter taste of what's sweet
I felt,
I feel,
the lash that lavishes; —
doubt;

the bitterness of the caress,
the time,
pass the time,
wait,
wait for her;
                    oh,
                          love
bitterness,
          bile flower,
          the un-honey,
pain of memory,
reminder of what's wanted;

I want: I don't have,
impossible to stop wanting

— all there is is my want;

the nontaste,
invisible sword in the body;
bile.

March 30, 1966

AD 1

Gôsto amargo do que é dôce,
senti,
sinto,
o chicote que fere,
acaricia;

dor,
amargor da carícia,
côrpo que queima —
dentro;

lembrança do prazer,
lazer do amor,
o que é,
o que será
, oh —
o querer
impossível deixar de querer,
fazer ou desfazer,
ser;

o amor,
espada que fere,
açucar que adoça —— ;
fel.

AD 30-3-60

Bitter taste of what's sweet,
I felt,
I feel,
the whip that wounds,
caresses;

pain,
bitterness of the caress,
body that burns —
inside;

memory of pleasure,
leisure of love,
what is,
what will be,
                    oh —
                              the want
impossible to stop wanting,
making or unmaking,
being;

love
sword that wounds,
sugar that sweetens — ;

bile.

March 30, 1966

Images

Figure 1. *Grupo Frente 093*, 1956. Courtesy Projeto Hélio Oiticica.

Prior to the turn toward participation in his work, Oiticica was known as a concrete artist. This painting is part of a series of gouache-on-cardboard pieces from the mid-1950s and is characteristic of Oiticica's work from the era. Like other concrete artists, Oiticica subscribed to an anti-representational mode of geometric abstraction that was interested in shape, color, and the plane. The name of this particular work, and the series to which it belongs, is a reference to the Rio de Janeiro–based group of artists known as Grupo Frente that included members such as Lygia Clark and Lygia Pape, along with Oiticica. At the end of the 1950s, members of Grupo Frente would go on to form the neoconcrete movement, spurring an increasing investment in participatory art.

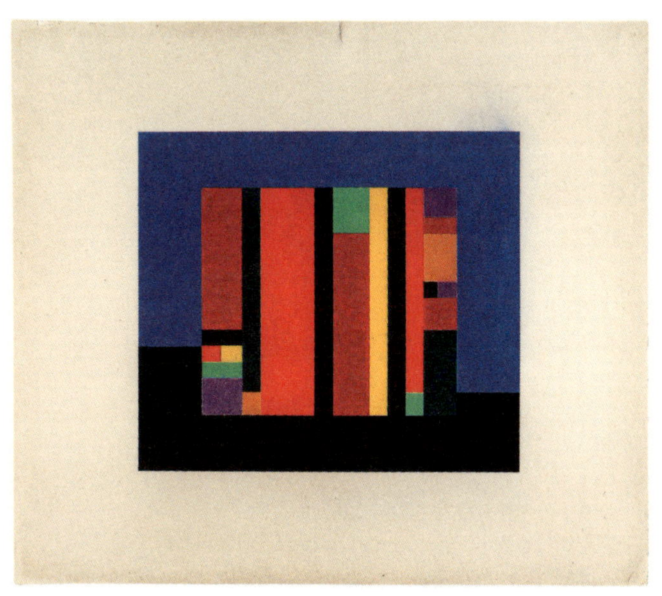

Figure 2. *Tropicália* (detail of poem by Roberta Camila Salgado: “dark sky / why don’t you clean and shine my world?”), 1967. Courtesy Projeto Hélio Oiticica.

Conceived of in 1966 and first displayed a year later, Oiticica’s *Tropicália* installation integrated numerous materials, including poetry. In this detail of the work, it’s possible to see one of many brief poems by Roberta Camila Salgado displayed throughout the installation. These were written directly onto objects such as pieces of stone and metal and sit in the rocky sand on which the installation’s additional materials rest. *Tropicália* is understood as a critical reappraisal of Brazil’s international image as a tropical paradise. The installation also included two *Penetrables*—PN 2 “Purity is a myth” and PN 3 “Imagetical”—whose structures call to mind Rio’s favelas.

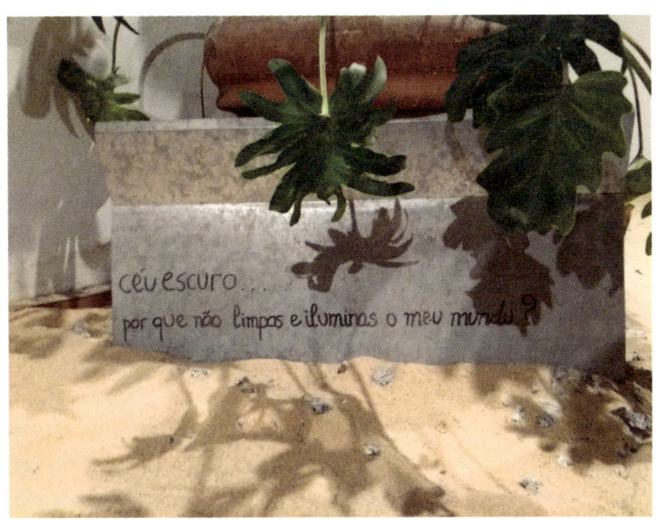
céu escuro...
por que não limpas e iluminas o meu mundo?

Figure 3. *B50 Bólide saco 2 "Olfático"* (B50 Fireball Sack 2 "Olfactic"), 1967. Courtesy Projeto Hélio Oiticica.

While writing *Secret Poetics* Oiticica was working on his *Bólide* (Fireball) series, which took the form of boxes, sacks, and other containers that viewer/participants would physically manipulate or engage with. This example brings out the relationship between the "smell" in the first poem of the collection and the sensory works in Oiticica's *Bólide* series that involve actual smelling/actual physical experiences. This "Olfactic" sack allows the participant to smell coffee beans contained in the sack through a plastic tube.

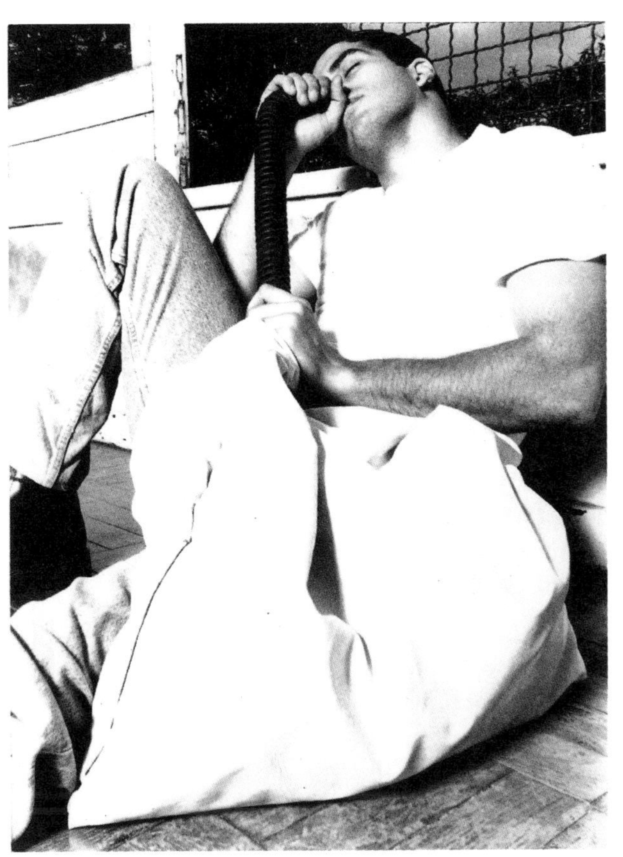

Figure 4. *B47 Bólide caixa 22 "Mergulho do corpo"* (B47 Fireball Box 22 "Plunge of the Body"), 1966–67. Courtesy Projeto Hélio Oiticica.

This water-filled basin is another example from Oiticica's *Bólide* series. Both this work and the "Olfactic" sack represent one way through which former neoconcretists attempted to cultivate intuition in art, in that participants would intuitively interact with the objects, and the experience of this sensorial interaction would be, itself, the art. The word *mergulho* (dive/plunge), along with a description of what could be the water-filled basin seen here, appears in *Secret Poetics* in 1964, which predates this work. As with the "smell" invoked earlier in the collection, the poetry verbally depicts an experience, while the works of art have the potential to make it actual.

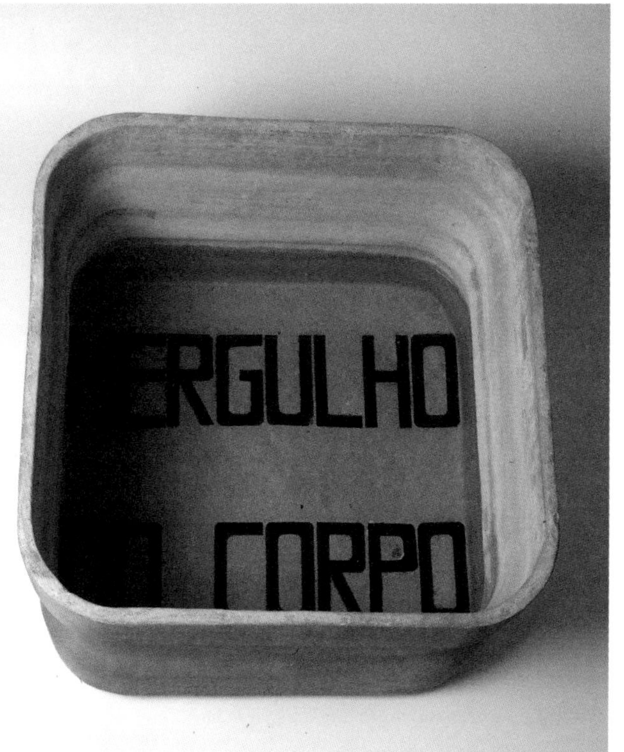
ERGULHO
CORPO

Figure 5. *Nildo da Mangueira vestindo P15 Parangolé capa 11 "Incorporo a revolta"* (Nildo of Mangueira wearing P15 Parangolé cape 11 "I embody the revolt"), 1967.
Courtesy Projeto Hélio Oiticica.

This well-known work by Oiticica is part of his series of wearable capelike *Parangolés*. This *Parangolé* is worn here by Nildo, a collaborator from the Mangueira favela and samba school in Rio de Janeiro with which Oiticica worked closely, particularly for this series. The embodiment and dance that this work invites relate to the images of dance and rhythm evoked in poems written in 1964. Here, the political resonance is increased by comparison with the poems, which fits into the timeline of the Brazilian dictatorship. It began in 1964, and increased in severity over the years, with 1968 marking the introduction of new, more punitive restrictions and increased state violence.

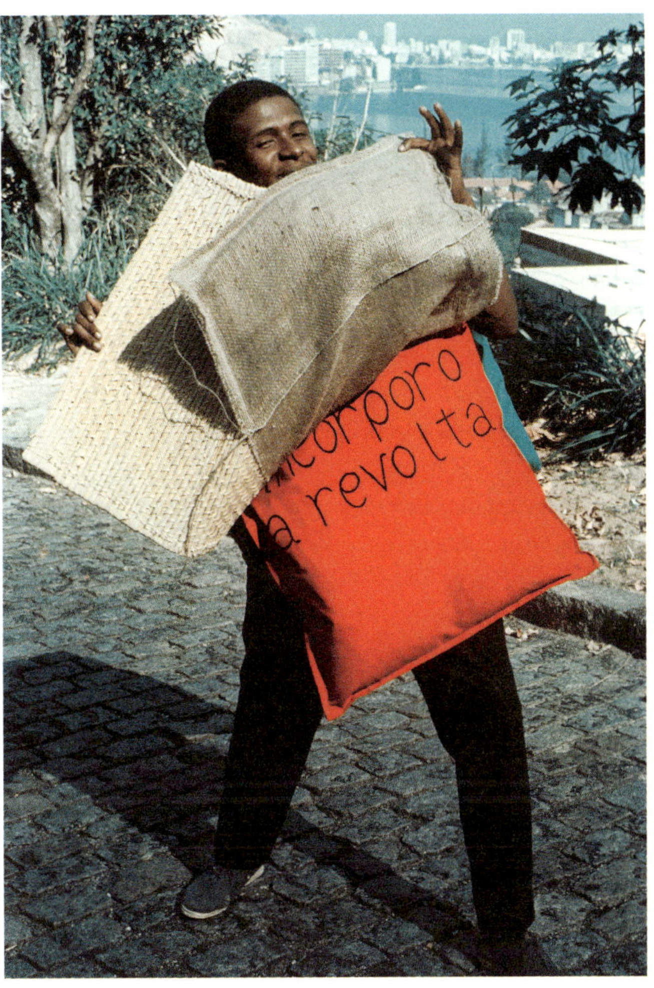
corporo
a revolta

Figure 6. Lygia Clark and Hélio Oiticica, *Diálogo de mãos* (Dialogue of Hands), 1966. Copyright © "The World of Lygia Clark" Cultural Association. Unknown photographer.

This work, made in collaboration with artist Lygia Clark (fellow member of Grupo Frente and neoconcretism), relates to the *mãos, / cruzar as mãos* (hands, / crossing hands) in the poem from March 22 of the same year. This is an example of the types of participatory works made by former members of the neoconcrete movement, who were interested in the Möbius strip, in part for its ability to abolish inside/outside binaries. *Dialogue of Hands* also relays the influence of French phenomenologist Maurice Merleau-Ponty on the post-neoconcrete participatory experiments: "When one of my hands touches the other, the moving hand functions as subject, and the other as object" (Merleau-Ponty, *Phenomenology of Perception*, 371). In the poem, the image of hands touching takes on erotic overtones, suggesting that a sexual encounter also has the effect of dissolving the boundaries between subjects and objects.

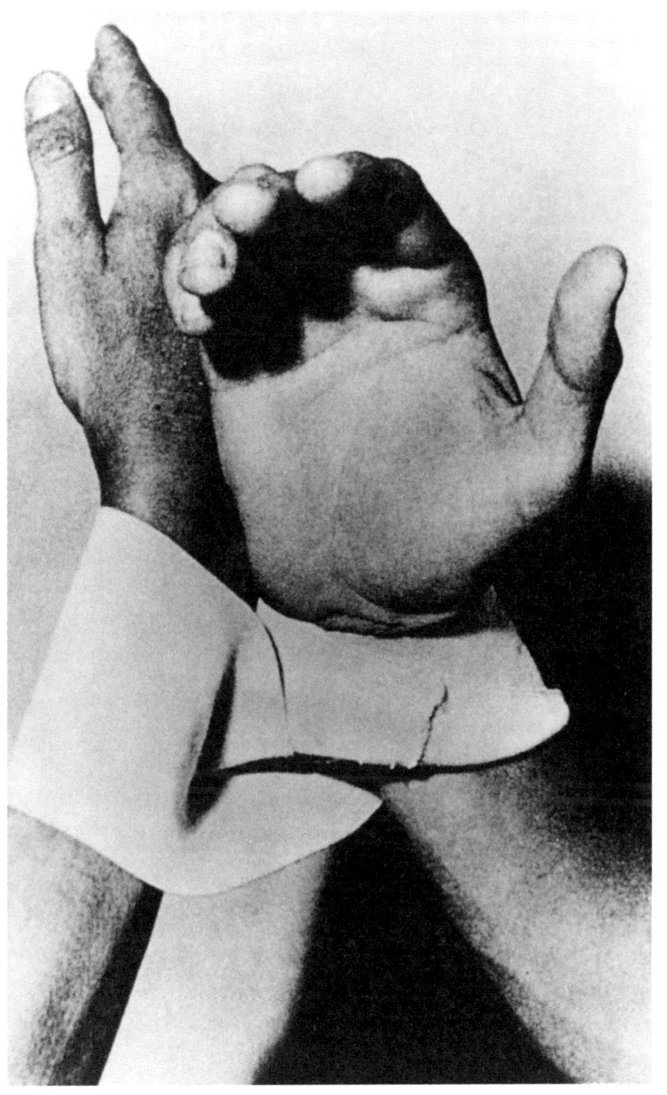

Figure 7. *B52 Bólide saco 4 "Teu amor eu guardo aqui"* (B52 Fireball Sack 4 "I keep your love here"), 1966–67. Courtesy Projeto Hélio Oiticica.

This image shows Oiticica demonstrating another work from the *Bólide* series. Several examples from this series include language that references love and endurance. The words inscribed on the bag, "I keep your love here," relate to the images of love, eroticism, and loss present, particularly, in the latter half of *Secret Poetics*. For instance, where the final poem meditates obsessively on lack and the bitter want for an absent love, this work, which "keeps" love, is both sentimental and a bitter reminder that the love that's being "kept" isn't physically there. The plastic sheath on which these words appear also echoes the eroticism present in the poems, evoking a condom or, given that the upper body is enclosed in this case, autoerotic asphyxiation.

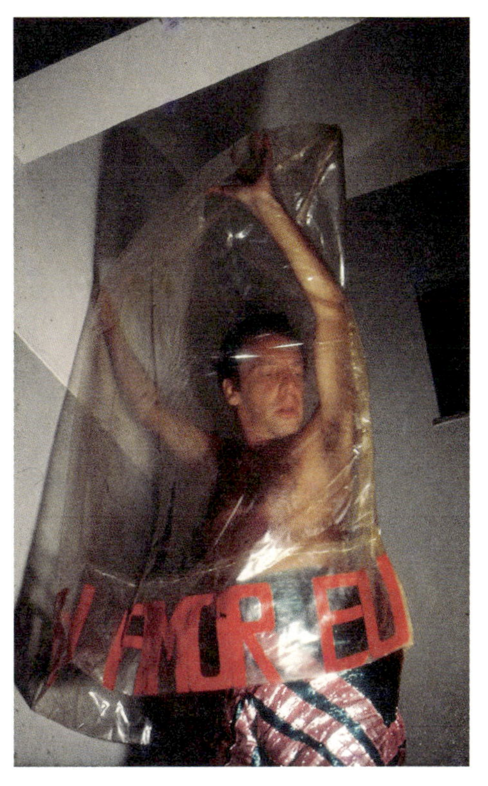
EU

Oiticica's Phenomenological Lyric; or, the De-intellectualization of Art

by Pedro Erber

The desire for a radical de-intellectualization of art underlies and motivates Hélio Oiticica's *Secret Poetics,* tying this brief incursion into lyric poetry to his long-standing creative trajectory. The meaning and reach of this task must be understood in relation to the transformations and predicaments of art in the 1960s.

The idea of writing poetry as an exercise of de-intellectualization might sound counterintuitive. The recourse to verbal communication in the art of the late 1960s has often been associated with a growing emphasis on conceptual, intellectual apprehension as opposed to a sensorial, materially based relationship to the artwork. What authorizes the claim that the opposite would be the case here? And, after all, if this brief experiment was in fact meant to fulfill such a critical task in Oiticica's lifelong artistic project, why would he declare it "secret"?

Secret Poetics—this brief series of poems written between 1964 and 1966 and left unpublished until long after Oiticica's untimely death in 1980—stands out as anomalous among the copious written documents in Oiticica's archive, not least for its ostensibly "secret" character. "Am I even supposed to be reading this?" one wonders, with a mix of guilt and voyeuristic curiosity. The unease about invading the artist's (and the individual's) privacy is compounded here by the very subject matter of the poems, full of descriptions of personal moments of self-discovery and allusions to sensual and sexual encounters.

The notion that this *Secret Poetics* might have been intended as an entirely private outlet, a kind of personal diary disconnected from Oiticica's public career as an artist, finds additional support in the poems themselves. Their lyrical and metaphysical themes seem somewhat alien to the developments of concrete poetry and its radicalization within the neoconcrete group, of which Oiticica was one of the core members. The contrast in tone with Oiticica's numerous theoretical and programmatic texts, as well as the inscriptions that permeate many of his visual artworks from the 1960s onward, is striking.

Yet, here and there, the reader stumbles upon clues of a closer connection between this "secret" poetic endeavor and the bulk of Oiticica's public, carefully documented, and theorized trajectory in the visual arts. As Rebecca Kosick points out, similar topics, ideas, and expressions appear contemporaneously in his visual works and poems, as most clearly exemplified in the case of the poem "Água / superfície vítrea / mergulho" and its dialogue with *B47 Bólide caixa 22 "Mergulho do corpo"* (B47 Fireball Box 22 "Plunge of the Body"—Fig. 4). Visual work and poem seem to echo, resonate, and at times even translate each other.

However, between his public artistic practice and his "secret" poetic writing—or as Oiticica himself described it, "the things I will express verbally, poetically"—the most significant connections are never straightforward. If some level of translation takes place between verbal and visual, between the plastic and the poetic, this operation is never what is primarily at stake. Neither are they entirely opposed to each other as one might be tempted to think—and as Oiticica himself suggests, in claiming that the lyrical, poetic expression is "the polar opposite of my plastic work." Rather, Oiticica enlists poetry to rescue visual practice from intellectualization. Poetic writing supplements plastic creation in its path toward de-intellectualization—an endeavor that is present throughout Oiticica's creative practice and that profoundly marks his position within the artistic panorama of the late twentieth century.

THE POETIC AND THE PLASTIC

I take "secret" here not so much as a synonym for personal or intimate, but rather as an indication of what should provisionally remain invisible, hidden, or unframed, like an exercise or creative essay meant as a preparation for something else. "'Secret' is what I want because I am not a poet," Oiticica writes, "although an urgent necessity leads me to verbal expression." Neoconcrete artists, despite their defiant attitude toward established conventions and their professed aim to blur the lines between artistic practice and everyday life, to eliminate the distance between artwork and spectatorship, were surprisingly mindful of the boundaries between poetry and the visual arts. The poet Ferreira Gullar, a founding member of the group and author of the "Neoconcrete Manifesto," once expressed this concern in relation to his own experiments with the material aspects of language, which came so close to the realm of the visual arts that he felt the need to cut them short, as he "didn't want to be a sculptor."[1] This almost instinctive respect for genre boundaries in no way contradicts the radicality of their experiments. On the contrary, it reflects the neoconcrete group's profound concern with the frame of artistic practice, its consciousness of the fragile identity of art outside the frame. And yet, just as the plastic element emerges organically from a kind of internal necessity in Ferreira Gullar's poetic trajectory, Oiticica's "urgent necessity" of verbal expression, too, arises out of his artistic project, rather than from a merely personal situation—even if the artistic and the personal become here inevitably intertwined.

Indeed, in describing the "polar opposition" between his poetry and his plastic work, Oiticica conveys already a strong sense of their mutual imbrication. Everything hinges upon the expression of the "immediate," the "fleeting," the supposedly "inconsequential" aspects of everyday experience. These constitute, according to Oiticica, the fundamental object of "true lyric," and thus the theme of his *Secret Poetics*. Poetry, he argues, eternalizes the fleeting, the immediate:

> The image,
> memory,
> the tactile,
> contact with the body.

---

1 Gullar, "Interview," 99.

Meanwhile, Oiticica writes, "My plastic work [is] all oriented toward an expression that excludes fleeting, inconsequential accidents," adding immediately, as if on second thought: "despite embracing them." Rather than mutual exclusion, opposition here indicates a mode of dialogue, of complementarity. In its "polar opposition" to his plastic work, *Secret Poetics* is part and parcel of Oiticica's creative project. Poetry is enlisted to restore the immediacy of everyday experience—which the plastic embraced but ultimately concealed and, thus, effectively excluded—and to preserve it, or as Oiticica puts it, to "eternalize" it: "what might be inconsequential, day-to-day, becomes experience and is eternalized in the poem." Capturing and eternalizing lived experience in its immediacy is the primary function of poetic writing: "What was, / stayed, / sediment of memory." And what called for this endeavor was the excessive intellectualization of artistic expression.

Mediating between art and poetry in Oiticica's trajectory, both biographically and in terms of the ontology of creation, is a crucial third term: namely, dance. Dance constitutes the hinge between the plastic and the poetic. The first comments on *Secret Poetics* that Oiticica makes in his notebook date from 1964, the same year in which he took up dancing and started participating in the samba scene in Mangueira, a favela on the northern side of Rio with a rich cultural legacy, home of one of the city's most traditional samba schools.

Back then, even more than today, Rio's favelas were rather unusual places for an upper-middle-class youth to hang out. Hélio's mere presence in Mangueira constituted an act of transgression of social barriers and class conventions. But, more than that, Mangueira was for him a quasi-mythical place of self-discovery, probably the site of his first homosexual experiences, and a continuous source of inspiration for his creative project. Samba was at the center of all that. Dance represented for him the quintessential site of de-intellectualization. About his experience with samba, Oiticica wrote in 1965:

> First of all, it must be clear that my interest in dance, in rhythm, samba in my case, came from a vital need for de-intellectualization, for intellectual disinhibition, from the need for free expression, because I felt threatened in my expression by excessive intellectualization.[2]

The need for de-intellectualization is, thus, both a "vital" one, a personal need for "intellectual disinhibition," and simultaneously an inherent necessity arising from the development of Oiticica's artistic expression—and, more broadly, from the historical trajectory of twentieth-century art. In fact, at this point, the artistic and the personal could no longer be separated. The excessive intellectualism of modern art had swiftly removed artmaking from the realm of feeling, of subjective expression, but also from sensorial

---

2 Oiticica, *Aspiro ao grande labirinto*, 72.

experience. This separation, and the neglect of the sensorial realm in the name of objective, rational creation, constituted the target of Oiticica's critique—a position that announced itself already in the 1959 "Neoconcrete Manifesto" in its denunciation of the "dangerous rationalist exacerbation" of concrete art.[3] To combat the excessive intellectualism of concrete art, its "tendency to an always greater rationalization of the principles of painting,"[4] constituted one of the neoconcrete group's explicit aims. Doing so without falling back into the subjectivist, romantic trends that had dominated the international art of the previous decade was one of the movement's crucial challenges.

DEMATERIALIZATION AND INTELLECTUALISM

Lucy Lippard and John Chandler famously described the transition from "anti-intellectual, emotional/intuitive processes of art-making," characteristic of the early postwar decades, toward the "ultra-conceptual art that emphasizes the thinking process almost exclusively," which predominated in the 1960s.[5] If abstract expressionism and other currents of informal abstraction set the tone of the international art world of the 1950s in an outburst of emotions and limitless freedom of

---

3 Gullar et al., in Aracy, *Projeto construtivo brasileiro na arte*, 80.

4 Ibid.

5 Lippard and Chandler, "The Dematerialization of Art," 46.

creative expression, by the end of the decade, minimal art emerged as a drastic curb on its excesses. And just when it seemed impossible for artistic expression to get any more sober, the late 1960s brought about further radicalization with the emerging trends of what would be called "conceptual art" or "idea art." Artists such as Sol LeWitt, Joseph Kosuth, Carl Andre, and others who congregated around the dealer-curator Seth Siegelaub, occupied the most cutting-edge New York scene with "dematerialized" works that suggested a purely intellectual relationship with art and sought to avoid sensorial distraction. Beyond New York City, analogous conceptual trends emerged contemporaneously in the work of a wide range of artists on the US West Coast, in London, Tokyo, and other urban centers around the globe.

As objects "dematerialized" and consideration of sensorial perception subsided in both the making and appreciation of art, verbal communication emerged as a central element in the "visual" or "plastic" arts. Swiftly rejecting aesthetic concerns as matters of taste and decoration, Kosuth's work embodied conceptual art in its purest, almost literal form. In the enlarged photostats of dictionary definitions that compose his *Art as Idea as Idea* series, the concept itself becomes the work. The relationship between word and thing, between word and idea, between word and writing, is the very stuff of artmaking understood as a process of increasing abstraction. "The dictionary works went from abstractions of particulars [like *Water*] to abstractions of abstractions [like *Meaning*],"[6] Kosuth writes in *Art after Philosophy*.

Kosuth's method presupposes a conception of writing as the most abstract medium of communication of ideas and concepts, the one with the least degree of sensorial intervention and appeal. Precisely this presupposition of the immateriality of writing, in the sense of the irrelevance of its material support for the communication of ideas, is what concrete poets in Brazil had been frontally attacking since the mid-1950s. Poetry, by definition, disproves the understanding of writing as a transparent means of expression, capable of pure intellectual communication. Concrete poets emphasized this intrinsic character of poetic writing by making the materiality of language one of the programmatic cores of their experimental endeavors. In doing so, they aspired to reach a level of "metacommunication," in which verbal and non-verbal communication coincide as a "communication of forms, of structure-content" rather than as a mere passing along of messages.[7] Diametrically opposed to Kosuth's use of language as a tool for dematerialization through abstraction, concrete poets attended to the sensorial traits of language—the potential for visual nuance and impact of writing, the tone and rhythm of speech—which the logical, analytical understanding of language fundamentally downplays and ignores.

---

6 Kosuth, "Art after philosophy," 30.

7 de Campos et al., *Novas*, 218.

Brazilian art in the 1950s and 1960s was certainly not immune to or insulated from the newest artistic trends that flooded the international market. Nonetheless, different chronologies in the circulation of visual works and ideas, not to mention specific political and cultural circumstances, rearranged many of the same trends and conflicts in a significantly different configuration. In contrast to Lippard and Chandler's observation and what took place in most cultural capitals of the developed world, artmaking in postwar Brazil was not dominated by "anti-intellectual, emotional/intuitive processes." Running counter to the prevailing international trend, the objective rationality of concrete art saturated the local art scene with its basic colors and geometric shapes. Abstract expressionism and other currents of non-geometric abstraction were certainly not absent from the Brazilian artistic landscape, but the most influential artists and critics remained staunchly averse to their privileging of individual, subjective expression over objectivity and reason in artistic creation.

In 1957, American curator and director of New York's MoMA Alfred Barr, acting as a juror for the Fourth São Paulo Biennial, notoriously disparaged the work of Brazilian avant-garde painters as "Bauhaus exercises." Responding to Barr's criticism, Mário Pedrosa, Brazil's foremost art critic, registered the dissonance between the local avant-garde and the international consensus in an article entitled "Brazilian Painting and International Taste." Pedrosa argued that Barr's dissatisfaction with

Brazilian art boiled down to the fact that some foreign critics "do not like to allow our artists modern research and a modern language that is not in accordance with current tastes in the main European centers."[8] Barr, who decades earlier had been among the first to introduce the Bauhaus to the American public, could only regard the Brazilian embrace of its constructivist aesthetics as an epigonic move. Ironically, however, if cool shapes and cold reason were out of fashion in New York in 1957, the following decade would bring them back with a vengeance.

Unsurprisingly, by the end of the 1950s, while North American artists were turning against the emotional subjectivism of Abstract Expressionism, Brazilian art moved, once again, in the opposite direction, with the proposal to reintroduce the sensorial dimension of lived experience in artmaking. Neoconcretism spearheaded this radical rupture with the intellectualist tendencies of the preceding generation. But the sharp break did not take the shape of a simple return to the privileging of subjective expression and individual emotions. Instead, neoconcretism walked the tightrope of a twofold rejection: on the one hand, of the excessive rationality of concrete art that permeated the Brazilian scene, and, on the other, the subjective irrationality of informal abstraction, which still ruled the international art world.

---

8 Pedrosa, "Pintura brasileira e gosto internacional," 280.

Here, too, dance provides an ideal model. The lived experience of dance, in its openness to the world, to the outside, the body's movement in harmony with the senses, the perception of rhythm: all this presents an entirely different path of de-intellectualization from the one that leads to introspection and the expression of individual sentiments.

the dance,
the cosmos, in rhythm

But long before Oiticica's vital encounter with samba, the neoconcrete movement encountered the phenomenology of Maurice Merleau-Ponty. Phenomenology provided Oiticica both a framework to understand the experience of dance and a basis from which to relate it to his own artistic project. More broadly, the "Neoconcrete Manifesto" and a significant portion of neoconcretists' theoretical and programmatic texts appropriated the language of Merleau-Ponty's phenomenology—perception, lived experience, embodiment—and shared its philosophical positions. Perhaps it was no mere coincidence that Merleau-Ponty was known as the best ballroom dancer in the Parisian postwar intellectual scene.

PHENOMENOLOGICAL ART

It is well known that Merleau-Ponty's philosophy came to play a significant role in the art of the 1960s worldwide, most famously in the work and writings of Robert Morris and others associated with minimal art. Colin Smith's translation of *Phenomenology of Perception*, published in 1962, introduced Merleau-Ponty to the English-language readership, deeply impacting the discourse of artists and critics in the United States. Meanwhile, in Brazil, his influence could be felt at least as early as the 1950s—partly because Brazilian intellectuals and artists could read French and thus had access to the original text independently of Portuguese translations, but also due to the significant penetration of Gestalt psychology in Brazilian artistic discourse since the early postwar years, which prepared the ground for the reception of Merleau-Ponty's thorough critique of disembodied, intellectualist perception.

At the center of the theoretical debate on perception in the Brazilian postwar artistic scene was Mário Pedrosa, whose 1949 dissertation *On the Affective Nature of Form in the Work of Art* first presented the theories of Gestalt psychology to the Brazilian art world—and who later introduced Merleau-Ponty to members of the neoconcrete group. These circumstances not only allowed them to engage with phenomenology significantly earlier than their US peers; most importantly, they enabled a more precise grasp of Merleau-Ponty's critical appraisal of Gestalt theory and sharper insight into the crucial stakes of his intervention.

Robert Morris has often been criticized for failing to distinguish between, and ultimately for conflating, phenomenology and Gestalt theory.[9] Indeed, the *Notes on Sculpture* make no effort to draw a line between Merleau-Ponty's usage of the term *Gestalt* in *Phenomenology of Perception* and its meaning within the context of Gestalt psychology. And yet, the difference between them, which can appear at first as a matter of terminological minutia, indicates one of the core insights of Merleau-Ponty's philosophy.

Merleau-Ponty inherited from Gestalt psychology the realization that our immediate perception of reality takes place first through whole forms or figures (both of which are possible translations of the German word *Gestalt*), from which we can later abstract individual elements, rather than by perceiving isolated particles first and later connecting them into increasingly complex forms. His crucial objection to Gestalt psychologists such as Max Wertheimer and Kurt Koffka, among others, pertained to the way they understood the nature of such patterns or forms. According to Merleau-Ponty, Gestalt psychology understood the figures or forms that mediate and enable our apprehension of things in the world as objective realities, that is, as existing outside and independently of our experience, thus falling back into what he called an "empiricist" view of perception. Against this notion, Merleau-Ponty described Gestalt

9 Andrew Chesner, for instance, argues that the problem with Morris's use of the word Gestalt consists in that it "conflated two sets of ideas, one from Gestalt psychology and the other from phenomenology." (Chesner, "Desublimating the Gestalt," 9.)

as a phenomenon inherent to human perception: that is, as something that belongs neither to objective nor to subjective reality, and that does not exist previously to or beyond the act of perception itself.

From early on, even before embracing Edmund Husserl's phenomenological method, Merleau-Ponty argued that an adequate understanding of human experience required a thorough critique of the traps of empiricism, on the one hand, and intellectualism, on the other. Empiricists, according to him, regarded the elements of external reality as the basis of human experience and, thus, understood experience mechanistically in terms of cause and effect; meanwhile, the intellectualist position, which Merleau-Ponty associated with Descartes and Kant, explained experience mainly in terms of mental processes, thus understanding phenomena as products of human consciousness.

According to Merleau-Ponty, both positions misunderstood the true nature of perception. As he puts it in *The Structure of Behavior,* "to do justice to our direct experience of things it would be necessary to maintain at the same time, against empiricism, that they are beyond their sensible manifestations and, against intellectualism, that they are not unities in the order of judgment, that they are embodied in their apparitions."[10] In his view, Gestalt theory, too, failed to provide an answer to this philosophical impasse. Its understanding of the role of forms or patterns (*Gestalten*) in perception managed to

10 Merleau-Ponty, *The Structure of Behavior*, 187.

shift the weight of Kant's intellectualist standpoint, from which it derived. However, as a psychology, Merleau-Ponty argued, Gestalt theory remained a "prisoner of the facts of science"; in understanding form as an attribute of the objective world, it could not avoid falling back into the empiricist position.[11]

While Merleau-Ponty is admittedly rather ungenerous in characterizing Gestalt theory as understanding form to be objectively existent, this characterization does help get his point across. More importantly, it highlights the shortcomings of the mid-twentieth-century artistic discourse's appropriation of Gestalt theory. To some extent, Merleau-Ponty's charge of "empiricism" may also be leveled at Pedrosa's 1949 thesis, which incorporates Gestalt psychology in discussing form as an intrinsic attribute of artworks, upon which relies his whole understanding of the educational power of art. Under such circumstances, it would not be too far-fetched to speculate that it was also Pedrosa's encounter with Merleau-Ponty, among other things, that later led Pedrosa to considerably reformulate his theoretical framework.

The "Neoconcrete Manifesto" incorporated Merleau-Ponty's critique of empiricism and intellectualism, albeit without thoroughly distinguishing between the two positions. Its fiercest attack is directed at the extreme rationalism and "mechanistic" understanding of painting that informed concrete art. But the authors

---

11 Merleau-Ponty, *Phenomenology of Perception*, 51.

of the manifesto reject, as well, the irrationalism of Dada and Surrealism. Instead, the text advocates an organic understanding of art, "not as a 'machine' or 'object' but as a quasi-corpus." The artwork, they argue, "might be decomposed in its parts through analysis, but it only gives itself entirely to a direct, phenomenological approach."[12] Most importantly, the artwork differs from a mere material mechanism insofar as it possesses a kind of "tacit" significance, a term that the manifesto explicitly attributes to Merleau-Ponty.

To argue about the tacit significance of art is to appeal to an aspect of artistic expression that cannot be apprehended by language, an element that precedes any form of linguistic communication. This is the realm of what Merleau-Ponty described, in *Phenomenology of Perception*, as a "tacit *cogito*" in opposition to the "spoken *cogito.*"[13] Because the artwork operates in this tacit dimension—even when it takes place in and through language—its mode of expression cannot be reduced to purely mechanical processes, as Gestalt theory might intend. This does not mean that artistic expression should be attributed or relegated to the realm of the irrational. The "tacit" realm is rather the not-yet-spoken, not-yet-rational, not-yet-conscious, which constitutes nonetheless the precondition of all rational, logical communication and simultaneously exceeds it.

12 Gullar et al., in Aracy, 80.

13 Merleau-Ponty, *Phenomenology of Perception*, 422.

Intellectualism, in its understanding of consciousness as entirely transparent to itself, is unable to account for this pre-conscious level of experience. And yet, this is the realm in which all lived experience takes place, before language and rational thought come in to make it conceptually intelligible. At least since the time of the neoconcrete rupture, an unrelenting desire to access and express this realm of human experience informs Oiticica's creative trajectory. For him, to de-intellectualize art did not mean to eliminate any interference of the intellect in artmaking or to propose an entirely feeling-oriented conception of art. Oiticica was certainly no anti-intellectual. It is important to differentiate here between intellect and intellectualism. While art is never entirely devoid of some level of intellectual activity, the problem with intellectualism consists in its inability to recognize and account for any aspect of experience, communication, expression that escapes the grip of logical, conceptual thought.

"THE BEAUTIFUL / CONCEPTLESS"

The de-intellectualization of art is also its deconceptualization. Nothing is more antithetical to Oiticica's project than Sol LeWitt's famous statement about conceptual artistic practice, "The idea becomes a machine that makes the art."[14] But not because Oiticica was opposed to ideas, concepts—or machines. Rather,

---

14 LeWitt, "Paragraphs on Conceptual Art," 12.

what this principle—and conceptual art by definition—excludes is the whole realm of what the concept cannot access or contain, that which exceeds the possibilities of logical expression: in Oiticica's words, the "fleeting," seemingly inconsequent everyday realm of experience. And this exclusion takes place not only in conceptual art strictly speaking but is an inherent tendency of the modern visual arts in general. As Ferreira Gullar puts it, "The artist searches in painting or in sculpture for a primary experience of the world, but painting itself (and sculpture, too) is already a conceptualized world, which is necessary to overcome."[15] Oiticica perceived this lack not only in the art of his contemporaries, but also in his own visual expression, and he turned to poetry to recuperate this primary experience.

This level of lived experience before or beyond conceptualization is the object of Oiticica's *Secret Poetics*. In contrast to the conventional understanding of lyric poetry, Oiticica's lyric is not devoted to the expression of subjective emotions or feelings. The lyrical "I" here is always already outside of itself, in contact with the world. More than an "I" who feels, it is an "I" who senses, touches, smells, and encounters—and, while doing so, attempts to preserve this experience in a kind of phenomenological lyric.

After the publication of *Phenomenology of Perception*, in 1946, Merleau-Ponty defended his theses in front of the Société française de philosophie. Reacting to

15 Gullar, "Diálogo sobre o não-objeto," 98.

Merleau-Ponty's conception of the inexorably localized, bodily character of perception and to his critique of empiricism, Émile Brehier objected that perhaps his ideas might be "better expressed in literature and in painting than in philosophy." "Your philosophy results in a novel," he added. "This is not a defect, but I truly believe that it results in that immediate suggestion of realities which we associate with the writings of novelists."[16] It certainly was a defect in Brehier's view—even if he sugarcoated the criticism in polite language. In fact, he went as far as openly wondering whether science would even exist today if "all philosophers had been phenomenologists since antiquity." At stake in Brehier's remark is a concern with the very survival and identity of science and philosophy as realms of questioning that intrinsically presuppose the separation between the subject and object of experience, and thus the possibility of objective knowledge. Phenomenology's radical challenge to this separation, its emphasis on the "primacy of perception," Brehier realized, puts in check the very distinction of philosophy and science in their purported relationship to truth. With that distinction abolished, gone would be also any possibility of a clear separation between philosophical and artistic discourse.

Conversely, excessive rationalism brings art too close to science and philosophy, to the point of effacing its specificity. The danger identified here is not a new one. In *The Birth of Tragedy*, Nietzsche decried

16 Merleau-Ponty, *The Primacy of Perception*, 30.

the destruction of great Greek art at the hands of "aesthetic Socratism," which dictated that only the rationally intelligible was truly beautiful.[17] In twentieth-century Brazil, concrete art fully embodied this Socratic ideal, considering art "as a means of conceptually deducible knowledge," as painter Waldemar Cordeiro wrote in the 1952 "Manifesto ruptura."[18] In the 1960s, conceptual artists would take this notion to an almost parodical extreme. Oiticica's aim in *Secret Poetics* is the complete opposite:

> Beautiful,
> the beautiful,
> conceptless.

Through rampant intellectualization and increasing distance from the sensorial realm, Oiticica realized, art risked losing itself in philosophical lands. De-intellectualization appeared then as a necessary measure to safeguard the limits of artmaking from dissolution into philosophical discourse.

Sensing the threat that haunted the art of his time, Michael Fried famously argued in 1967 that "the success, even the survival, of the arts has come increasingly to depend on their ability to defeat theatre." In *Art and Objecthood,* Fried described the experience of time

17 Nietzsche, *The Birth of Tragedy*, 62.

18 Cordeiro et al., in Aracy, *Projeto construtivo brasileiro na arte (1950–62)*, 69.

as duration inherent to minimal art, or as he preferred to call it, "literalist" art, as "paradigmatically theatrical" in contrast to the immediate "presentness" of modernist art. The crucial stake that animates Fried's passionate and pious tone reveals itself in the essay's last sentences: "We are all literalists most or all of our lives. Presentness is grace."[19] Precisely because "we are all literalists most or all of our lives," because duration constitutes our basic experience of time, art can only distinguish itself through absolute presentness, its identity consisting in a kind of secularized religious experience. For Oiticica, too, at stake was the existence and identity of art as art. But he sensed that intellectualism rather than theatricality was the foe—that the survival of art depended on its ability perhaps not to defeat, but to sidestep philosophy.

19 Fried, "Art and Objecthood," 9.

Bibliography

Amaral, Aracy A., ed., *Projeto construtivo brasileiro na arte (1950–62)*. Rio de Janeiro: Museu de Arte Moderna, 1977. Exhibition catalog.

Amor, Monica. "From Work to Frame, In Between, and Beyond: Lygia Clark and Hélio Oiticica, 1959–1964." *Grey Room* 38, Winter (2010): 20–37.

Bachmann, Pauline Medea. "A poesia como subtexto: A inscrição corporal da Poética secreta de Hélio Oiticica." *Remate de Males* 39, no. 1 (2019): 171–90. https://doi.org/10.20396/remate.v39i1.8653999.

Brett, Guy. *Kinetic Art: The Language Of Movement*. London: Studio-Vista, 1968.

Campos, Haroldo de. *Novas: Selected Writings*. Edited by Antonio Sergio Bessa and Odile Cisneros. Evanston, IL: Northwestern University Press, 2007.

———. "Tradition, Translation, Transculturation: The Ex-Centric's Viewpoint." Translated by Stella E. O. Tagnin. *TradTerm* 4, no. 2 (1997): 11–18.

Chesner, Andrew. "Desublimating the Gestalt. Towards an Archaeology of Robert Morris's Anti Form." *Zeitschrift für Ästhetik und Allgemeine Kunstwissenschaft* (ZÄK), Sonderheft 19 (2021): 1–30.

Clark, Lygia, and Hélio Oiticica. "Lygia Clark and Hélio Oiticica: Letters 1968–69." Translated by Michael Asbury. In *Participation: Documents of Contemporary Art*, edited by Claire Bishop, 110–16. Cambridge, MA: M.I.T. Press, 2006.

Coelho, Frederico Oliveira. "Livro ou livro-me: Os escritos babilônicas de Hélio Oiticica (1971–1978)." PUC-Rio, 2008.

Erber, Pedro. *Breaching the Frame: The Rise of Contemporary Art in Brazil and Japan*. Oakland, CA: University of California Press, 2014.

Fried, Michael. *Art and Objecthood: Essays and Reviews.* Chicago: University of Chicago Press, 1998.

Gullar, Ferreira. "Diálogo sobre o não-objeto." In *Experiência neoconcreta: Momento-limite da arte*. São Paulo: Cosac Naify, 2007.

———. *Ferreira Gullar in Conversation with = En conversación con Ariel Jiménez.* New York: Fundación Cisneros, 2012.

———. "Interview" by Fernando Cocchiarale and Anna Bella Geiger. In *Abstracionismo geométrico e informal: A vanguarda brasileira nos anos 50*. Rio de Janeiro: Funarte, 1987.

Katz, Vincent. "Living Colour: Hélio Oiticica." *Tate Etc.*, no. 10 (2007). https://www.tate.org.uk/tate-etc/issue-10-summer-2007/living-colour.

Kosuth, Joseph. “Art after philosophy.” In *Art after Philosophy and After.* Cambridge, MA: MIT Press, 1991.

LeWitt, Sol. “Paragraphs on conceptual Art.” In *Conceptual Art: A Critical Anthology*. Edited by Alexander Alberro and Blake Stimson. Cambridge, MA: M.I.T. Press, 1999.

Lippard, Lucy and John Chandler, “The Dematerialization of Art.” In *Conceptual Art: A Critical Anthology,* edited by Alexander Alberro and Blake Stimson. Cambridge, MA: M.I.T. Press, 1999.

Lisson Gallery. “Press Release Hélio Oiticica.” London: Lisson Gallery, 2022.

Masseno, André. “Os poemobjetos de Roberta Camila Salgado: Criação e materialidade.” *Elyra,* no. 17 (2021):: 179–98. https://doi.org/10.21747/2182-8954/ely17a12.

Merleau-Ponty, Maurice. *Phenomenology of Perception.* Translated by Donald A. Landes. New York: Routledge, 2012.

———. *The Primacy of Perception.* Edited by James M. Edie. Evanston, IL: Northwestern University Press, 1964.

———. *The Structure of Behavior.* Translated by Alden L. Fisher. Pittsburgh, PA: Duquesne University Press, 1983.

Nietzsche, Friedrich. *The Birth of Tragedy and Other Writings.* Edited by Raymond Geuss and Ronald Speirs. Cambridge, UK: Cambridge University Press, 1999.

Oiticica, Hélio. *Aspiro ao grande labirinto*. Rio de Janeiro: Rocco, 1986.

Pedrosa, Mário. "Da natureza afetiva da dorma na obra de arte." In *Forma e percepção estética. Textos escolhidos II.* Organized by Otília Arantes. São Paulo: EDUSP, 1995.

———. "Pintura brasileira e gosto internacional." In *Acadêmicos e modernos. Textos escolhidos III.* Organized by Otília Arantes. São Paulo: EDUSP, 1998.

"Penetráveis, 1961-1980." Museu de Arte Moderna Rio de Janeiro. Accessed June 10, 2022. https://mam.rio/obras-de-arte/penetraveis-1961-1980/.

Small, Irene V. *Hélio Oiticica: Folding the Frame*. Chicago: University of Chicago Press, 2016.

ACKNOWLEDGEMENTS

I am grateful to Lucas Nunes Vieira for our conversations about this book as it progressed and to Pedro Erber for thinking with me about Oiticica for many years, and still. Thank you to the World of Lygia Clark for permission to share Clark's collaborative work with Oiticica here. My deepest thanks, as well, to Ariane Figueiredo of the Projeto Hélio Oiticica and to César Oiticica for their support of this project and generous stewardship of Hélio's work. Thank you to Julia Klein, Matvei Yankelevich, the Bristol-Brazil Centenary Fund, and the Fundação Biblioteca Nacional, for your support in bringing this book to life.

Rebecca Kosick
Bristol, England
May 2023

HÉLIO OITICICA (1937–1980) is among twentieth-century Brazil's most significant artists, with a multifaceted practice that included painting, sculpture, installation, performance, filmmaking, and writing. Oiticica was a leading member of Grupo Frente (an association of concrete artists) and, in 1959, co-founded the neoconcrete movement with artists and poets including Lygia Clark, Lygia Pape, and Ferreira Gullar. Oiticica was a 1970 Guggenheim Fellow, and today his work is held in collections across the world, including at MoMA and the Tate Modern.

REBECCA KOSICK is a poet, translator, and co-director of the Bristol Poetry Institute at the University of Bristol (UK) where she is also Senior Lecturer in Comparative Poetry and Poetics. Kosick is the author of the monograph *Material Poetics in Hemispheric America* (Edinburgh Univ. Press) and the poetry collection *Labor Day* (Golias Books), and her poems and translations have appeared in literary venues such as *The Recluse*, *Fence*, and *The Iowa Review*. She was born in Michigan.

PEDRO ERBER is Professor of Comparative Literature at Waseda University, Senior Research Associate at Cornell University, and Editor of *ARTMargins*. He is the author of *Breaching the Frame: The Rise of Contemporary Art in Brazil and Japan* (UC Press).

Typeset in Heldane, a renaissance-inspired serif designed by Kris Sowersby for Klim Type Foundry, and Zirkon, a contemporary gothic designed by Tobias Rechsteiner for Grilli Type. Designed and typeset at Winter Editions. Printed and bound in Lithuania by BALTO print.